A Teen Yearbook

My Life in My Own Words

By April Rogers

U-TALK PUBLICATIONS

"Where your voice counts"

Akron, Ohio

A Teen Yearbook: My Life in My Own Words
Copyright 1998 April R. Rogers
ISBN 0-9643763-5-0

Revised Edition of the My Teen Years Memory Journal
First published in 1993

Printed in the United States of America

Published by:
U-Talk Publications
Post Office Box 1266
Akron, Ohio 44309-1266

Designed by: DUNN + ASSOCIATES
Hayward, Wisconsin

Thank you for purchasing A Teen Yearbook!
We welcome your comments.
Please submit to address listed above.

A Teen Yearbook

My Life in My Own Words

This book belongs to:

_____

From:

_____

Date:

_____

Age:_____   Grade: _____

CONTENTS

CONTENTS

All About Me

My friends would describe my personality as: _____

_____

_____

_____

_____

My best feature is: _____

The thing that is most unique about me is:_____

_____

_____

The physical traits that would describe me are: _____

_____

_____

I am most proud of: _____

_____

_____

My best daydream is: _____

_____

_____

_____

_____

_____

My worst nightmare is: _____

_____

_____

_____

_____

_____

If I could be anything I wanted to be, I would: _____

_____

_____

_____

I enjoy helping other people by: _____

_____

_____

I get spending money from: _____

I do most of my shopping at: _____

_____

The things I buy most often are: _____

_____

_____

Some things on my wish list are:

_____

_____

All About Me

My idea of a perfect day is: _____
_____
_____
_____
_____

I am most grateful for: _____
_____
_____

To me God is: _____
_____
_____

My place of worship is: _____

I have grown spiritually this year by: _____
_____
_____
_____

If I could do one thing to change the world, I would: _____
_____
_____

In my spare time I like to: _____

_____

_____

Things that make me happy are: _____

_____

_____

Things that upset me are: _____

_____

_____

My biggest pet peeve is: _____

_____

Something I would like to improve about myself is: _____

_____

_____

My birthday is on: _____

I celebrated my birthday this year by: _____

_____

_____

_____

_____

_____

_____

Photos

Photos

My Family

My parents' names are: _____
_____

My siblings' names are: _____
_____

We spend time: _____
_____
_____
_____

My family would describe my personality as: _____
_____
_____

The way I feel about my family is: _____
_____
_____

We have fun when we: _____
_____
_____
_____

The best thing about my family is: _____

_____

_____

The most unique thing about my family is:_____

_____

_____

Major changes that occurred in my family this past year were: _____

_____

_____

_____

Sometimes we disagree about: _____

_____

_____

We could improve how we: _____

_____

_____

Favorite family memories: _____

_____

_____

_____

_____

_____

_____

_____

Photos

Photos

Special Friends

My closest friends are: _____

_____

_____

They are special to me because: _____

_____

_____

The traits I admire most in each of my friends are: _____

_____

_____

We have fun when we: _____

_____

_____

_____

The most important qualities in friendship to me are: _____

_____

_____

The friend that I've known the longest is: _____

We have known each other for _____ years

My friends and I laugh about: _____
_____
_____

We talk most often about: _____
_____
_____

Our favorite hangout is: _____

They influence me by: _____
_____

I influence them by: _____
_____
_____

We encourage each other to: _____
_____
_____

Memorable moments: _____
_____
_____
_____
_____
_____
_____

Photos

Photos

That Special Someone

(fill in this person's name in the appropriate blank spaces provided)

_____ is special to me because:

_____

_____

_____

We first met at_____ on _____

When I'm around _____ I feel _____

_____

_____

Places we visit: _____

_____

We have fun when we: _____

_____

_____

_____

I remember the time we:_____

_____

_____

(That special someone can be a loved one, friend, someone of the opposite sex,
or anyone who is special to you)

Photos

School Stuff

Grade: _____

School: _____

City & State: _____

Principal's Name: _____

School Colors: _____

Mascot: _____

Best Subject: _____

Worst Subject: _____

Favorite Classes: _____
_____

Favorite Teachers: _____
_____

Awards/Honors: _____
_____

Clubs I belong to: _____
_____
_____

Positions I hold: _____

_____

Sports I play: _____

_____

Most embarrassing school moment: _____

_____

_____

Cafeteria buddies: _____

_____

Funniest school moment: _____

_____

_____

Memorable moments: _____

_____

_____

_____

_____

_____

_____

_____

_____

_____

My Goals

My goals for the year _____ and the action steps to help me accomplish my goals are:

Accomplished

1. _____ ☐

   Action steps   1. _____
                    2. _____
                    3. _____
                    4. _____
                    5. _____

Accomplished

2. _____ ☐

   Action steps   1. _____
                    2. _____
                    3. _____
                    4. _____
                    5. _____

Accomplished

☐

3. _____

Action steps   1. _____

2. _____

3. _____

4. _____

5. _____

Accomplished

☐

4 _____

Action steps   1. _____

2. _____

3. _____

4. _____

5. _____

Accomplished

☐

5. _____

Action steps   1. _____

2. _____

3. _____

4. _____

5. _____

(Action steps are those things you need to do that will move you closer to accomplishing your goal)

My Favorite Stuff

My Favorite Book: _____

My Favorite Author: _____

My Favorite Movie: _____

My Favorite Actress: _____

My Favorite Actor: _____

My Favorite Sport: _____

My Favorite Athlete: _____

My Favorite Song: _____

My Favorite Singer: _____

My Favorite Music Group: _____

My Favorite Food: _____

My Favorite Beverage: _____

My Favorite Restaurant: _____

My Favorite Hobby: _____

My Favorite Hangout: _____

My Favorite TV Show: _____

My Favorite Color: _____

My Favorite Phrase: _____

My Favorite Time of Day: _____

My Favorite Activity: _____

My Favorite Type of Music: _____

My Favorite Holiday: _____

My Favorite Season: _____

My Favorite Teacher: _____

My Favorite Class: _____

My Favorite Magazine: _____

Signs of the Times

People & Things that are HOT this year of: _____ are:

Movies: _____
_____

Actors/Actresses: _____
_____
_____

Television Shows: _____
_____

Singers/Music Groups: _____
_____

Dance Steps: _____

Hairstyles: _____

Sports Figures: _____

Clothes/Shoes: _____
_____
_____

Price Tags

The average prices of the following everyday items
this year of: _____ are:

Movie Ticket $ _____

Compact Disk $ _____

Jeans $ _____

Cassette Tape $ _____

Hamburger $ _____

Newspaper $ _____

Tennis Shoes $ _____

Hair Cut $ _____

Concert Ticket $ _____

Candy Bar $ _____

Gallon of Milk $ _____

Fashions

(Place pictures of this year's hottest fashions on this page)

Fashions

(Place pictures of this year's hottest fashions on this page)

Fashions

(Place pictures of this year's hottest fashions on this page)

Fashions

(Place pictures of this year's hottest fashions on this page)

Special Events

Special Event: _____

Date: _____ Place: _____

Theme: _____

Significance of the event: _____

_____

_____

Who attended with me: _____

_____

What I wore: _____

_____

Who was there: _____

_____

_____

Highlights of the event: _____

_____

_____

_____

_____

_____

Special Events

Special Event: _____

Date: _____ Place: _____

Theme: _____

Significance of the event: _____

_____

_____

Who attended with me: _____

_____

What I wore: _____

_____

Who was there: _____

_____

_____

Highlights of the event: _____

_____

_____

_____

_____

_____

Holidays

My favorite holiday of the year is: _____

because: _____

_____

I celebrate by: _____

_____

_____

Other holidays that I celebrate are:

Holiday: _____

I celebrate by: _____

_____

_____

Holiday: _____

I celebrate by: _____

_____

_____

Holiday: _____

I celebrate by: _____

_____

_____

Holiday: _____

I celebrate by: _____

_____

_____

Holiday: _____

I celebrate by: _____

_____

_____

Holiday: _____

I celebrate by: _____

_____

_____

Holiday: _____

I celebrate by: _____

_____

_____

Holiday: _____

I celebrate by: _____

_____

_____

Holiday Photos

Holiday Photos

Vacations

Vacation Spot: _____

Date(s) traveled: _____

Who went along: _____

_____

How I got there: _____

I stayed at: _____

What I saw & did: _____

_____

_____

_____

_____

_____

The most memorable thing about this vacation was: _____

_____

_____

_____

_____

_____

_____

_____

_____

_____

Vacation Photos

Vacations

Vacation Spot: _____

Date(s) traveled: _____

Who went along: _____

_____

How I got there: _____

I stayed at: _____

What I saw & did: _____

_____

_____

_____

_____

_____

The most memorable thing about this vacation was: _____

_____

_____

_____

_____

_____

_____

_____

_____

Vacation Photos

Around the World

The following events occurred around the world during
this year of: _____

Event: _____ Date:_____
Major details:_____
_____
_____
_____

Event: _____ Date:_____
Major details:_____
_____
_____
_____
_____

Event: _____ Date:_____
Major details:_____
_____
_____
_____

Event: _____ Date: _____

Major details: _____

_____

_____

_____

Event: _____ Date: _____

Major details: _____

_____

_____

_____

Event: _____ Date: _____

Major details: _____

_____

_____

_____

Event: _____ Date: _____

Major details: _____

_____

_____

_____

10 Years From Now

I plan to be:

Living in: _____

Employed by: _____

Attending or have graduated from: _____
_____

Driving a: _____

Dating/Engaged/Married? To: _____
     (circle one)

I plan to have accomplished the following: _____
_____
_____
_____
_____
_____
_____

Someday, (perhaps it'll be more than 10 years from now) I would like to have a total of _____ children

Class Trip

Grade: _____Teacher's name(s): _____
_____

Where we went: _____
_____

The chaperons were: _____
_____

We traveled by: _____

What we saw and did: _____
_____
_____
_____
_____
_____

The most memorable thing about this trip was: _____
_____
_____
_____
_____
_____

School Dances

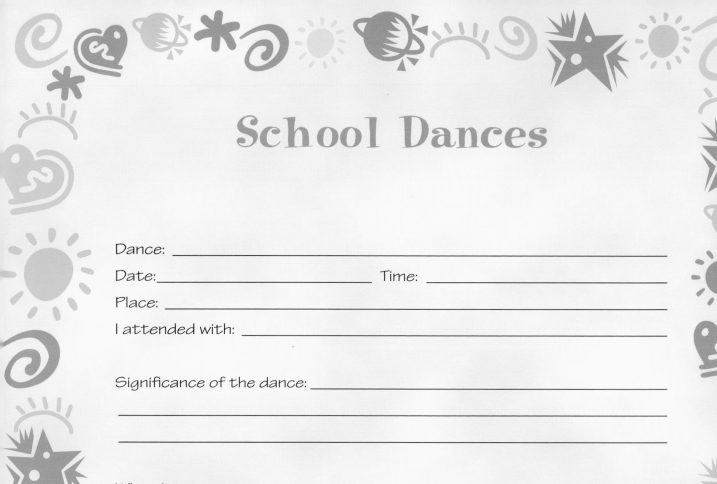

Dance: _____

Date: _____ Time: _____

Place: _____

I attended with: _____

Significance of the dance: _____
_____
_____

What I wore: _____
_____

Who was there: _____
_____

Activities after the dance:
_____
_____

Highlights of the dance: _____
_____
_____
_____

Photos

School Dances

Dance: _____

Date: _____ Time: _____

Place: _____

I attended with: _____

Significance of the dance: _____

_____

_____

What I wore: _____

_____

Who was there: _____

_____

Activities after the dance: _____

_____

_____

Highlights of the dance: _____

_____

_____

_____

Photos

Clippings

(Tape or paste school newspaper clippings, concert ticket stubs,
school dance tickets, etc... onto this page)

Clippings

(Tape or paste school newspaper clippings, concert ticket stubs,
school dance tickets, etc… onto this page)

New Discoveries

New Discoveries

Birthdays

My birthdate: _____

Name: _____ Date: _____

Name: _____ Date: _____

Name: _____ Date: _____

Name: _____ Date: _____

Name: _____ Date: _____

Name: _____ Date: _____

Name: _____ Date: _____

Name: _____ Date: _____

Name: _____ Date: _____

Name: _____ Date: _____

Name: _____ Date: _____

Name: _____ Date: _____

Name: _____ Date: _____

Dates to Remember

Date: _____ Significance: _____

_____

Date: _____ Significance: _____

_____

Date: _____ Significance: _____

_____

Date: _____ Significance: _____

_____

Date: _____ Significance: _____

_____

Date: _____ Significance: _____

_____

Date: _____ Significance: _____

_____

Date: _____ Significance: _____

_____

Photos

Photos

Autographs

(Have your friends & classmates autograph and/or
write a cool message to you on this page)

Autographs

(Have your friends & classmates autograph and/or
write a cool message to you on this page)

Autographs

(Have your friends & classmates autograph and/or
write a cool message to you on this page)

Autographs

(Have your friends & classmates autograph and/or
write a cool message to you on this page)

We sincerely hope that you have fun writing down your own thoughts, feelings, and experiences for this year of your teenage years in **A Teen Yearbook**. We would love to hear from you! Please drop us a note and tell us who you are!

Name_____

Address_____

City _____

State_____ Zip _____

If you are unable to find **A Teen Yearbook** at your favorite bookstore or gift shop, please feel free to order additional copies by sending a check or money order for $19.95 + $4 shipping & handling for each book (Ohio residents add 5.75% sales tax — $1.15 per book).

To: U-Talk Publications

           P.O. Box 1266

           Akron, Ohio 44309-1266

Be sure to include your name and mailing address with your order.

Thank you!